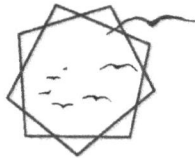

REVIEWS

Ann Rayburn's *Midnight Gardener Chronicles* is an enchanting, insightful tapestry of personal, family and historical reminiscences crafted in a lyrical tone and rhythm. As a memoirist and family therapist, I am fascinated and touched by the writer's reflections about the complexity of family relationships, the fragility of the parent-child bond, in particular; and the creation of myths and secrets to divert our attention to less painful thoughts and feelings. The line *Fragile roots above a fault line* from the piece "Leaning Against His Knee" touched me deeply. Our vulnerabilities lie just beneath the surface. The author relates how her aunts and other family members served as surrogate parents to mitigate the emotional distress created by loss and to enhance her self-esteem. From "Alice" she writes, *Of all the aunts, she taught me best how to live on my own, my best way.*

Midnight Gardener Chronicles portrays both the fragility and tenderness of life's journey. As the expression goes, "In the end is the beginning." Rayburn's piece "January" affirms our resiliency and offers us hope: *Like Buddhist monks on a mountain we fall down and get up ... tough as buried seeds, starting over in January.*

—Porter G. Shreve, Jr. author of *In Our Father's House*

Precarious as rock climbing and wondrous as the afterlife scene set by put-upon aunts playing canasta when the poet's problematic mother arrives, *Midnight Gardener Chronicles* unfolds the joys and sorrows of extended family and how Ann Rayburn deals with the human condition.

—Karren L. Alenier, author of *The Anima of Paul Bowles*

The
Midnight Gardener
Chronicles

The
Midnight Gardener
Chronicles

POETRY AND PROSE

ANN RAYBURN

The Midnight Gardener Chronicles: poetry and prose
Copyright ©2015 Ann Rayburn

ISBN: 978-1-940769-32-5
Publisher: Mercury HeartLink
Printed in the United States of America

Author photos by Turner Bridgforth

Cover: "Woman Pilgrim", sculpture by Debra Fritts.
www.debrafritts.net.

Contact the author at:
awrayburn@aol.com

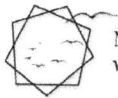

Mercury HeartLink
www.heartlink.com

UNGROUNDED

ROOTS AND FAULT LINES

SEEDS, THE SOWING

UNEXPECTED RAIN

SLIVERS OF GREEN

GOOD OMENS IN BONES

ACKNOWLEDGMENTS

Clerestory Press: "Under Leo"   Reprints: "Newcomers" ("The Landing"), "Rising and Converging," "Scavenger Hunt"

Federal Poets: "Why She Asks Him to Stay"   Reprints: "Deep Hour," "Debris" ("Housecleaning"), "Survival Guide," "Under Leo," "The Way Things Ought to Be"

Frantic Egg: "The Way Things Ought to Be," "Rising and Converging"

Passager: "Deep Hour," "Home Town," "The Moon Without a Pen," "Street Scenes, San Francisco"

Poetry Society of Virginia: "Adrift on the Inland Sea"

Poet Lore: "Going Under," "Intersections," "Housecleaning"

Potomac Review: "Survival Guide"

WordWrights: "Scavenger Hunt"

"Anthem," Leonard Cohen, "More Best of Leonard Cohen" Sony Music Records Entertainment, 1997

"Not Lie Down," Dougie MacLean, "Who am I" Dunfield Records, 2001

My Thanks

First, to the members of my poetry group of some eight years, Myra Bridgforth, Kirsten Hampton, Caroline McNeil and Mel Snyder, for their support, encouragement and helpful comments during our years together. Special thanks to my family for providing the initial spark for this book at my 80th birthday gathering in the mountains, and to Jeremy for so wisely and thoughtfully fanning the spark.

Many thanks as well to my memoir writing group, Kay Bean, Judy Bowes, Bea Epstein, Davye Gould, Martha Horne and Susan Post, with gratitude for their friendship, support and companionship as we've explored our various histories.

Thanks to teachers over many years at the Writer's Center in Bethesda; and to the Lost River Retreat Center in West Virginia, for the grace and quiet it provides writers and artists as we work to create beauty and meaning. Finally, my gratitude to the memory of Hilary Tham, a poet and mentor no longer with us.

And many thanks to Debra Fritts for use of her sculpture "Woman Pilgrim" on the cover. *www.debrafritts.net.*

To my sons Christopher and Michael,
and their families: Marianne, Kyle and
Mileah, and Lori, Kelsey and Colvin;
and to Jeremy

Deep Hour

What if when we say *Once upon a time*, the time
that it's upon is *now*? We sit for hours
at the lake's edge, watching birds and sky

flicker on the brink of dusk. If we asked children
what they know of time, before they're taught
to believe in clocks, they might complain about

time's corners: supper in a distant room, bedtime
a dead end to the day. They might report that
they've discovered *never*, then dance the shapes

of *forward* and *backward*, learned while rocking
in their mother's chair. We imagine their time
as being loose as sand, endless ripples

by the scalloped edge of the sea. Each day
an ocean away What I ask of time is this: to let
the lakeside almond trees blossom into flames again.

UNGROUNDED

Longitude

In August heat, the urge to be misplaced
can find you standing on the sidewalk, disoriented,
holding someone else's photos by mistake.
Trying to place *that* cottage, *that* sandy porch.
Before you know it, the drink's in your hand,
those are your ankles crossed on the railing.

This started years ago on autumn evenings.
Walking down the sidewalk, past windows
newly lit, you watched the figures gather:
the woman in the kitchen, the children at their books.
You set yourself among them, as if the man
had turned in his chair to gesture you inside.

This same impulse can make you want
to walk into the Tuscan landscape
on the museum wall, or marry the hero
of this month's novel, raise his grateful children.
No use wondering if you were carried off
by gypsies. You know someone's mislaid
the life you meant to live.

Adrift on the Inland Sea

Sky darkens to the sheen
of old pewter, thick trees hang
over still water. Our wrists,

resting on the oars, are light
as drowsy birds. Remember how

it feels to dive, touch grass
on the bottom. Waves of silk,
bubbles tapping our skin

like questions. The lake carries
our boat in its palm, light years away
from the tents on the shore.

Their shapes whisper with sleep.
Dreams rise from beneath their skins,
great moths flying to the moon.

Balancing Act

The first time you took me climbing
I almost cursed you, watching me from the ground,
belaying me. *There's a nubbin to your left* you said.

Clack of carabiners, rough sigh of rope on stone,
my breath, and right up against the rock, my heart.

Three quarters up its face, sweating, looking
down and afraid I might be sick, I thought it would
serve you right if I fell. Giddy at the top, I let you
teach me to rappel. Leaned back against cool air,

looked up at you, trusted your hands on the rope.
Then I stepped and bounced, even danced across the rock.

I thought of Superman and Lois in the movie – you know,
the scene when he takes her on a moonlit flight
across the city and beyond. She's nestled on his back
wearing a gown, something loose that almost tangles

with his cape. If he'd asked, she'd have made love
to him in an instant. Instead they dared to stay in flight.

It looked so easy in the movie. Like climbers seen
from a distance, surefooted on a narrow ledge. No close up
trails of sweat, no gauging when to step, hold on, let go.

Trusting Rope

Because only
the man who laid
the strands
to twist or braid
knows how many
fibers it holds.

Because each
strand contains
its springy nature
in the bending
when it's stretched.

Because
its frayed bristles
like wintry trees
against
a sleeping hill.

Because rain,
hard blown,
strikes the ground
like nine-tails.

Because it can be
turned upon itself
until it becomes
half-clove
sheet bend

bowline
cat's paw.

Because
its resting coils
become
the seagull's
labyrinth.

JANUARY

Over and over
the two-faced god
teases with hope
stings with regret.
Over and over
we promise, pledge,
resolve. Like Buddhist
monks on a mountain
we fall down and
get up, fall down
and get up.
Here is the snow
again, and so are we.
Dougie MacLean sings
*"You can fall but you
can't lie down."* Tough
as buried seeds,
starting over in January.

Sunday Morning, Baltimore Hotel

At one reflecting window, a woman
rests her hand on glass, watches
squares of light unfold across the rooftops.

Twenty-three stories below, orange cones
surround a steam pipe fitted to a street vent.

Frost-white steam escapes, twists above
the asphalt in wind-whipped braids.

She wonders if her watching is a pushing
or a beckoning. A flash: a woman in a red coat

swirls past raw dirt at an excavation pit
where blocks and pipes are stacked like toys.

Pigeons swerve and bank in unison.
White wings paint a checkerboard on bricks.

Behind a nearby door, a shower's soft
staccato drums the tiles, mimics her pulse

as she takes in with her palm the red,
the orange, the flatness and the feathers,

the geometric light outside which doesn't
know she's here, doesn't see her claim this day.

I Don't Ask Where You've Been

just as I didn't tell you, on that August night,
that I meant to write your life.

A full moon sliced its white blade down
the surface of the creek. Across dark water,
migrants' tents in shadow, rising sparks from campfires.
Guitar chords, laments in Spanish
we'd not learned in school.

You were the teenage king of gypsy dreamers:
a river boat, scribbled notes, a misplaced map.

When I don't know what to do I'll write
old Albert Schweitzer and ask him
what comes next.

Laughter, sparks into ash, fading voices.
I wonder where you've been.
My fingers still recall the back of your neck,
the shape of your mouth.

THE MOON WITHOUT A PEN

The moon wants to write its own haiku,
three lines uneven as its surface. It envies
the orange, whom it sometimes resembles,
for its failures of sentimental rhyme.
The moon draws a cloud across its eye,

weary of watching the boy and girl embracing
by the lake, the shining paper lanterns strung
above the pavilion. I once lost track of the moon
for months. The fat Egg Moon of April,
July's Thunder Moon pounding on its anvil,

all slipped by invisible as wind. At last, a coppery
Hunter's Moon arrived, its shadows racing us
as our sleds squeaked down fresh-packed snow,
then hissed across a frozen pond.
The man I was with got drunk on moonlight,

then on wine and the fire's warmth, and picked
a stupid fight. He later swore he'd never do that again,
but he did. The moon breaks its promises one
by one, slices through the crust of love,

leaves the craters burning. If the moon had
a pen and fingers to hold it, a poem would scroll
across the sky, about its own rough birth. About
how it feels to be the Long Night Moon,
rising, separate, in the winter dusk.

Now The Gardener Listens

The air is dense with sparks of pollen. The gardener,
accompanied by questions, bends to pull up witchgrass, tugs
at burdock, greets a world gone green as malachite.

She lets her thumb lick dirt that has stuck beneath her nails.
On the bricks, two ants, one black, one red, battle in the sun.
Red holds black by the throat, bends a toxic tail raised to
sting. Black shakes his foe as if to tire him, then drags him
down to a steep and gritty nest.

The gardener folds fresh dirt around young roots. Hears the
singing lapis sky, bees that roam among the vinca. Watches
a male chase, the female spurn, until at last
she's folded blossom-deep.

He dives. Then coupled they shoot up past budding trees,
as if to ride the contrail, swan-white and shining high.
The sun hangs like a blinding clue.

The air moves in currents around astilbe plants, as if
set in motion by beating wings. At the edge of the yard
a rabbit, resigned to its death, curls in the teeth
of the ginger cat who streaks to a hole in the fence.

Now the gardener listens, feels time embrace, hears
the lessons in the soil. This world demands persistence
of seed and leaf and hand.

Roots and Fault Lines

Scavenger Hunt

No really, the cousins murmur,
thank goodness we've reached the age
when we're not accumulating.
We're discarding.

We are gathered at my half-sister's house
after her funeral, after the memorial
consumption of tea and sandwiches,
the old stories retold.

A week later they are back
in a borrowed van, filling empty boxes.

It's not just something for nothing,
the half-used box of note cards,
an odd serving piece, the scatter rug.

We become cunning as Medieval bishops,
slipping relics under our vestments,
a shin bone here, a bloody scrap or tunic
there. We line up to touch the reliquary
that holds the blackened thumb,
hoping we've outsmarted time.

I do not begrudge the cousins
their brimming boxes, the world of things
that saves them from our recent whiff
of death. I see them revitalized as old
warriors, ingesting their enemies' hearts.
If we're eating we must still be alive.

INHERITANCE

When I found them on the shelf
by your jewelry box,
I felt a prick of recognition:
Six fat diaries, five years each.

Mine now, because I had seen one of them
years before when you, gossiping with guests,
looked up some detail of a long ago
college football weekend.

I thought, *I want to read those books some day*.

Bulky, thick with words, they are like the diaries
I once kept. Covers locked with tiny keys, as if
anything that fragile could protect our secrets.

Dear Frances, eldest child of our father, child
of the wife who died, here are the maps you left,
the shape of the world I entered.

My Tarot card-reading aunt would point
to my Piscean chart, loving secrets, would say
I was born with a voyeur's eye.

I say we were meant to be joined,
by a father's blood, by ink.

FRANCES STARTS HER DIARY

She was a "girly girl" before the phrase was coined,
hair bow big as a swan, white knee socks,
ankles neatly crossed. Even then she was industrious
as a queen bee, recording each day's games, who spoke
to her or didn't, what she read each night.

When she wrote her first lines at twelve
I was twelve years away from birth. We shared
only a father's genes. Now I've become
the keeper of these fattened volumes, thirty years
of entries in her miniscule script.

January 16, 1922. Teased Mabel and Aldwyn
most of the day. Did not have my button hole
for sewing class.

She began, and I read on.
Someone would find them, she knew.

COMING SECOND

Bellevue Ranch, dusky in its shady grove
               of eucalyptus trees. Dances at the lake,
each entry chattier than the last. Dear Frances,
               you're telling me
about your eighteenth year, hugging the world
               with your sun tanned arms.
About college boys who followed you
               down the San Joaquin from Berkeley.

Then. May 21, 1928: *Mother riding with Mrs. Hunter.*
          Mother on Bandero & thrown.
          Bina & I took her to hospital.
          Still unconscious with hemorrhage of the brain.

Stop. Breathe. I was not expecting it so soon.
          To the hospital off & on. Seems better but unconscious.
          Dad called & San Francisco doctor coming down.

Look out the window. Then, at what comes:
          Early morning Mother passed away.
          Doctor said basal fracture of the skull.
          All to Nana's in San Francisco - many people.

It is May here, too. All green with bursting sprouts.
For months I've read your words, not thinking
               of where you were bringing me.
She died and our father fell in love again
               and suddenly I was possible.
Owing my existence to a stumbling horse
               and your terse grief.

Iowa Portrait in Sepia

They are downcast, my mother and her siblings, mute,
remembering angry voices like the scratchings of a hoe.
They've trudged here in the wake of one more argument,
pointless as dust. They begrudge the photographer,
the lighted studio.

He gives the girls carnations, hoping they'll reveal
the smallest smile. Studying the sepia print, we see
two brothers flanking three sisters. My mother's flower
lies untouched across her lap.

At home their father waited, where he'd plowed his shape
into the sagging couch, held his balding head and sulked.
See, my mother says to me, *see how from our faces
you can guess the stories none of us would speak aloud?*

Living It Twice

I knew before I read Fran's diaries that my father was twenty years older than my mother, that he was widowed two years before they met. I knew that his first wife was killed in a riding accident, and that Fran was his eldest child by that marriage, born in 1910. I knew a son, Richard Jr., was born in 1915. Frances was eighteen when her mother died; she was just five years younger than my mother. When her widowed father married my mother, Fran wasn't told of their elopement; she read about it in the newspaper. Both my mother and Fran were beautiful, socially active, somewhat willful and used to having their own way. How did they maneuver around one another?

I learned of Fran's diaries when I visited her during my college years. I too had once confided my daily life to a diary. Like Fran, I left hidden-in-the-open clues about myself in them. When I wrote I sometimes felt as if I were reliving my life for some unknown future purpose. I tore up my younger volumes before I married in 1958, but probably not before my mother had read them.

An Unexpected Lesson

I am about six years old, standing with my mother on the back steps of our apartment building in San Francisco. The steps adjoin those of the apartment of my mother's closest friend, Madge, a divorcee with a son named Jerry. Madge is painfully informing my mother that I have called her son an insulting name – probably 'spoiled brat' because that is what my mother has called him. My mother apologizes on my behalf and with embarrassed firmness insists that I too apologize to Jerry and to Madge.

As I do this I arrive at a new realization: I feel betrayed by my mother – she knows perfectly well where I heard that description of him. At the same time she and I suddenly become allied in a new partnership, maneuvering in the tricky arena of unspoken adult negotiations. We have become a team of two, and I'll be expected to understand her often silent instructions for how to survive in our world.

Street Scenes, San Francisco

We moved to the apartment when I was four,
left the house with the wide porch
and the rock garden. The new street rose
forever narrow, steep, tilting into shadows.
The building's door, ornately grilled
like all the others, one more confusion.
Up the slow elevator, down the hall, never sure
what we'd find behind our door. Outside the kitchen,
grey stairways down to the garden strip
where my mother willed her fuchsias to grow. Inside
my father withered, became a ghost. Below us,
storage lockers, the dark cement corridor
of my nightmares, where I ran, legs pumping, going
nowhere, when I wasn't dreaming of riding
in a runaway truck, skidding backward down our hill.

Today, a lifetime later, we've come to this old mansion
to see Wayne Thiebaud's art. Not his shiny pop art
frosted cakes. I want these visions he painted
of that city. His landscapes hover, just as memory does.
They hang like arrows shot from somewhere in midair.
His streets dive, plummet and pitch forward
off the edge of canvas, toward uncertain space,
or perhaps it's only down to the next corner
where they'll level off, laser-straight, safe between
chalk-white buildings. Next he tips us into darkness,
night a deep fissure. Tall buildings, narrow crystals,
mica specks for windows. *I get queasy when I look at them*

too long, a young boy smiles to his father, who then explains
perspective: *Pretend you're looking down disappearing railroad tracks.*

Thiebaud's angles bend my sight, crack open
the old steep stairway. Never mind that
half a century later, I've seen how that street
defies my memory: its slope has eased, broadened
to catch the western sun in polished windows.
It's become the kind of street newcomers might seek
if they arrive by choice, not in flight.
Still I want to tell the boy, *You've got it right,*
I lived on those streets, and they will drive you dizzy
if you let them. I wonder if he's learned
to save himself in airborne dreams at night.

In them we can fly, slip between crystal buildings
like a fugitive kite. We can hold our dream-breath,
forget what our senses know, as if the daylight world
didn't matter, as if it had no matter of its own.

Leaning Against His Knee

Row after row of numbers
feather-soft across the page:
I watch the carbon tip
of his draftsman's pencil:

I am a mesmerized four year old
in a gentle fugue,
unknowing.

How he'd sit, pretending
to be working on a job
that wasn't there. My mother
kept their old bargain:
went shopping, spent the money
that wasn't there,
dressed for dinner.

Fran's words:

May 19, 1939   *wrote letter to Dad telling him*
                          my thoughts . . . got it to Dad by
                          messenger . . . but no response.

July 24, 1939   *Dad . . . still afraid to talk to me.*

August 11, 1939   *Saw Dad - and hope I am*
                          in good standing now.

Fragile roots above a fault line.

Why My Father Didn't Fight in World War I

On our cruise up the Inland Passage to and through Alaska in 1994, Frances told me that according to family lore our father and his first wife, Fran's mother, returned to the West Coast mainland from Alaska, where he was working as an engineer, in order to for him to enlist; there an Army doctor told him he had only six months to live. Fran said he later told her there had been a *mixup with someone else's medical records.* I wondered if he had a similar near-escape story to explain why he never graduated from U. C. Berkeley, though according to my own mother he usually said, or let people assume, that he had completed his engineering degree there. Fran told me this earlier story with no sign of discomfort.

CROSSING THE RIVER

The trick is
 to stay
in motion

spot
the next
rock

one foot landing
one knee raised
to spring

 touch down

spring again

until you move
in cadence

with
water

until
your body
skims

above it

outrunning
shadows

NEWCOMERS

Wind brings news
of the sea. It carries the whine
of a gull, mutterings of sand
scratching at the shore.

Wind has pushed
our canvas sails, brine-stiff,
across rough waters. We are
strangers on these alien rocks.

No messages wait on papers
splayed and scattered
in weedy ditches, cross-hatched
by wheels and footprints.

We search new faces,
read them like clocks:
what time is it
in the land we left behind?

Resentful of the natives'
churlish optimism, we cannot
find beauty in wispy grass
lifting and falling in the wind.

We step over flotsam, walk
single file to the edge.
Across the buckled grey of the sea,
a ship, winking its lights, withdraws.

Seeds, the Sowing

Not Quite Refuges

That year Judy Garland sang
"Have Yourself a Merry Little Christmas."
Next year all your troubles will be far away.
My mother, my little sister and me.
Far from the city we'd known.
Troubles, still.

Not quite refugees, but something like them,
arriving at that dark house in the flat hot valley.
House of my mother's brother, where we crept
from my father's collapse, the divorce.

Among things lost, sold, discarded,
our old Christmas decorations. Aunt and uncle,
four cousins, cheerful and intact, never meaning
to be cruel. Rowdy dinner table set for nine. We three
speaking softly. Overwhelmed.

Hair in braids, satchel in my arms, each morning
I walked with the cousins. Six blocks past
match box rows of stucco houses to
Our Lady of Mercy school. Its red tiled roof

hunkered over newly studied truths.
Calls and responses of the Baltimore Catechism.
My mother, somewhere in the five square blocks
of downtown, lost to an office job. In that dark house
we spent four years parsing the fine distinctions
between escape and exile.

Home Town

Among those dusty trees, our parents
turned us loose to grow like weeds along the creek.

The handsome high school football star
groped girls in front of his friends, then
moved on to pose for Marine recruitment posters.
Told us before he left, *It's a good town
to come from, but it's no place to come to.*

Little known fact: before he went to Hollywood
and created Perry Mason, Earle Stanley Gardner
opened his first law office here.

One summer night our pastor died in a rectory fire,
pulled nearly fleshless from a tangle of empty bottles.
Did he ever miss the town he'd left in Ireland?

Old-style air conditioners cooled our houses.
Fans blew across dampened pads of felt,
pushed cool air through the rooms. Outside, below
the fans, we planted pungent mint, let the drain drip
water on it day and night. Winter mornings were dense
with tule fog. Under the orchard trees, smog curled out
from smudge pots, blanketing buds from frost.

Closer to town, between the endless rows of beans
and tomatoes, irrigation canals drew ribbons
across the land. Farmers' sons took time out
on dates, drove home to turn the spigots, redirect

water among the fields. Their tanned arms, resting
on open car windows, lured us girls up
and down the main drag, caught us wanting something,
thinking should we, could we, until
one by one we rushed to find the road out of town.

The Aunts: Agnes
Hell's Bells

My mother's sisters, Agnes and Cecelia, became surrogate mothers to my younger sister and me, not without bad feelings among all three. Agnes became my refuge, my comfort, my role model. We shared books and reading, long summer days in the cabin at Strawberry Lake, earthy not-quite-polite activities such as eating drippy ripe tomatoes over the sink like an apple. She was my source of praise and of tenderness. When I was raising my sons I often asked myself *What would Agnes do?* She had raised three very different and successful sons. *Hell's bells and little fishes* would come to mind, to be repeated as needed – those were her only cuss words and I probably used them more than she did. She loved us all for who we were, not for what we'd accomplished, but I suspected that I was special.

The Aunts: Cece

Learn politeness from the impolite.
Confucius

In her white Cadillac, after Sunday Mass, Cece gave us rides to the newsstand where she bought us a candy bar of our choice. She took these opportunities to share the wisdom of many elders with us, including Confucius, whom she greatly admired. At heart an archivally devout Catholic, she kept a scrapbook of pictures and articles about the various popes who reigned in mid-20th century. When she was widowed in middle age with no children, she began dating, making up for time lost when she was young. If she'd had a busy Saturday night she might stop by the local private ambulance service, where the owner would give her a reviving whiff of oxygen on her way to Mass. She believed in auras, extrasensory perception, and the intercession of saints in human affairs. When she gave us her oft-repeated quote above by Confucius, she wasn't just reminding us of rules, giving advice; it took me many years to realize that she was introducing us to strategy. She was more intelligent than she was allowed in those days to understand.

THE AUNTS: ALICE

Lovely Cobwebs

Alice was my father's younger sister. She was at family gatherings when I was very young, but my real connection with her came about through frequent weekend visits when I was in college. As we sat eating dinner on one of those early visits she remarked, *I'm going to keep those lovely cobwebs up on the ceiling, at least for a while. Don't you think they look nice there?* Neither of us picked up a duster all weekend. Alice had one adult daughter from her early marriage. Her husband had committed suicide before I was born, another bit of family history I only learned of from Fran's diaries. She and I read voraciously side by side. She was an avid gardener, and she loved the physical work as much as the landscape she created.

When I visited in those days she lived in a small cabin in the woods on the side of Mount Tamalpais, in Marin County. She was good friends with the gay couple in the cabin next door. She, too, told me things I hadn't known about my father. She was a free spirit in the world. Of all the aunts, she taught me best how to live on my own, following my own best way.

The Zombie Lullabies

Lake frogs quiet. Aunts reading, sewing in the cabin.
Tent house, squat and still, stars looking down through pines.
Bed big enough for nine, on the open porch.

Our eldest cousin, dark-eyed, deep-voiced, the chosen
storyteller. The younger eight of us, pajama'ed, under
blankets, a litter wrapped in flannel cocoons.

Flashlight held to morph a scary face – under the chin,
between the lips. Or tilted skyward, summoning a werewolf.
Now come ghosts that prowl across a distant moor,

rattling chains. A mirror shatters to the far off cries
of disappearing children. Cold fingers touch ankles.
Whose hand is that?

At story's end, whose turn to leave the warm bed first?
We shiver off to camp cots, sleeping bags,
warm bricks wrapped in paper. Darkness in the shelter.

Rock and Lake, Holding

Sapphire set in granite, fed by springs
thick with fern and columbine. Cloud-shaped
boulders, fat as Buddha's belly. Razor-thin
wakes of water skippers along the shore.

Wood needs chopping for the stove, clothes
to be washed in an iron tub. Warm bricks
wrapped in flannel to warm our beds. Stars
wheel through spiky clearings in the pines.

By the lake we pump our nut-brown legs
in a race on the hard dirt path. Our bare feet
make no noise. When we slip them into water

we walk on silky grass. Tadpoles slide
across our toes, slippery pebbles.
On certain days we traverse a narrow trail,

boards cantilevered to form a track along
the rock face. When we descend we'll sail
across the lake, no sound but the lap of water
at the bow, the slapping of the jib.

At dusk the Dipper ladles sky, bullfrogs
pound the air.

Someday we'll bring our children
on a pilgrims' hike around the lake. They'll
mutter about how far they have to walk.

On the farthest shore we'll find
a phone booth by the path, firecracker red,
unexpected as an alien's craft.

Our War

In San Francisco during the early days of the war, I learned to tape blackout shades to our apartment windows. My mother trussed me up in splints and bandages when she was studying to become a Red Cross volunteer. Later, with my cousins in Merced, we watched newsreels at the Saturday matinees. We learned new words for places we'd not thought about before: Mindanao Trench in the Pacific Ocean, Spitfires and Messerschmitts in the sky over Europe. Most of the fathers we knew were not drafted; they were needed at home or had too many children to qualify. Because we were on the western edge of the country, we feared the Japanese. We watched war movies and speculated about what would happen to us if they invaded. We played war games in vacant lots, brandishing cap pistols and rifles. We took reluctant turns being Japanese or German soldiers.

The owner of the small grocery store at the corner of G Street and 26th, half a block away, had a distinctly Germanic last name. We kids made jokes about him until our parents overheard us and told us to *cut that out. That's not how Americans talk about people.* After dinner I often wandered into our back yard victory garden, watching the miniature ditches my uncle had dug fill with water, then spread like slow rivers betwen rows of tomatoes and carrots.

THE WAY THINGS OUGHT TO BE

On good days our mother was elegant
as a spray of tulips in a silver bowl,
nodding slightly toward the sun.
Her monologues at dusk glowed
of cigarettes and scotch, amber
like her hair, reflected in the glass
that rolled across the linen table cloth

as if to join the smoky jars, the scent
of roses on her dressing table.
In good times we loved the weekly ritual:
the changing of her purses
shaken out above the bed, tumbling
coins, hankies, powder, combs.
Polished nails brushed tobacco flakes
from counterpane to floor.

We understood the goodness of sharp
corners on freshly sheeted beds, of notes
with monograms, pleats beneath hot irons,
herbs arranged by alphabet. In matching
pinafores and blouses, we set out her shoes
by her bed, lined them up like soldiers
waiting for the next command performance.

MOTHERSONG

Asleep, you would sometimes cry out,
while I dreamed of peaches, their heavy juices
sweet enough to dissolve a stone.

I had little enough in common with you –
dark hair to your spun wheat, a tendency
to slouch, creating uneven hems –

We never spoke of the man who started
it all, then left us, carrying God knows
what memories of your blue eyes.

In the kitchen we fought over forks
and peelings, grease behind the stove.
Carried our fears like rations

from room to room. Where did you keep
your tears? Folded under summer clothes?
In the box of spools by the sewing machine?

BOBO

He was an Iowa farmer with no land to cultivate, no livestock to tend, no blizzards to shovel through. My mother sometimes called her father 'the old gentleman,' striving for something gracious and respectful to say. We grandchildren called him Bobo. Over six feet tall and lanky, he walked with his bones jiggling under his overalls. Our main dealings with him were at holiday gatherings, when we pestered him to take out his false teeth and clack them at us. When he was an old widower he lived with Agnes and her family. More clackings, but these were about his behavior. He'd pee in the sink. He went to a few teenage beer parties with my cousins. He snuck liquor from my mother's closet when he came to water our lawn. When he was ninety-four, the police brought him home to Agnes when they found him driving down fog-bound Santa Fe railroad tracks. Agnes told me he'd sometimes sit on the edge of his bed at night, too tired to pull off his shoes, fighting tears, mumble I just want to die and go to heaven and be with Mayme.

Weeds

This is how news breaks loose from the basement
where it's been locked up: an Easter Sunday brunch,
my sixteenth year, an aunt and uncle in the kitchen.

She rinses plates. Arms crossed, he leans against
the cabinet, says to her, *I didn't know Dick died
in a mental institution.* A cousin carries in a bowl, pauses.

My mother has left the party, sits weeping
in a bedroom upstairs. *I told him not to tell. This family
can't let anything alone.* They are talking about my father.

Like dandelion seeds the words will drift
and catch in hair and pocket, move along the ley lines
of our clan. Each new shoot growing the story.

It was her way of protecting someone.
I will never ask her why she never told me
where he'd gone.

At The Gates

Under celestial trees, my aunts play canasta.
Their grace and wit restored, they look down to nod
at friends, some waving back from sterile sheets.

Then see my aunts' consternation when my mother arrives –
she who borrowed their lacy slips and boyfriends,
she the blonde to their chestnut coloring – floating
toward them on her cloud of Shalimar and Pall Malls.

Who am I, a chestnut child like the aunts, to say
that blondes aren't more deserving? Even though
I once was told that she sat up in her sickbed
to reject their bowls of chicken soup.

Now she's waving her sacramental cigarette at them,
looking for a light. At heaven's gates my aunts
rise up like drawn and flaming swords.
They demand the return of lacy slips.

Unexpected Rain

CANNERY, SUMMER, L954

Rubber-gloved and hair-netted, I stand at an endless
belt of peaches, steamed, peeled, split, pitted.

I nestle each in my palm, lop off its bruises
and chop it into two-inch chunks. Above us hangs

a cat's cradle, a braided mesh of belts and gears.
Beyond the corrugated walls, a rotting sweetness

lifts from slurry pools. Through the noise I slant
my eyes toward strutting forklift drivers. They flirt

with the nervy girls who curse in front of foremen,
go out at night for beer. I think of this week's paycheck:

lipstick, notebooks, bobby pins. I slice a peach, think
of words to cut from last night's poem. Discarded
lumps of gold.

INTERSECTIONS

In a dream I have forgotten, two people
approach a corner. I am looking down at them,
as if descending in a plane,

spying on the quilted town below.
I am here to retrieve myself
from stucco houses, from alleys that wind

among them. Heat rises from the streets,
stirs thin leaves on oleanders. Giant
sprinklers move across alfalfa fields.

A boy in a bomber jacket, musky
with leather and Juicy Fruit
used to whistle down this sidewalk.

I waited for him, wearing new lipstick:
Cherries in the Snow. In one of the stucco
bungalows a man sips coffee,

watches sparrows at the feeder.
If he goes out, will our paths cross at
that blind corner? Which of us will speak?

Why She Asks Him to Stay

Because she once saw
her mother's pale scalp
in lamplight, bowed,
waiting for sleep, only
her own thin bones for
company, and the late night
radio talk show.

Because in the morning
she met her mother's eyes
above the solitary bowl
and spoon, saw the rows
of home-canned jellies,
peaches, beans.

She wants him there at night
among the fallen ashes,
the books and dishes, a messy
life beside her own.

A carved moon watches
the darkened room,
where she needs his body
to curve around her like the shore
of a sheltering bay,
on their pale sea of sheets.

Stymied

by one another's

    hesitation

suspended between   the wishing

    the doing

one foot outstretched   one digging in

      (or maybe caught?)

the wedging of the soul   between

      two rocks

    the neither / nor of the unused ticket

      the word unwritten

the unsought lesson

    how to drown

in nothing

    meanwhile   the rain

      on fallen leaves

Evidence Disposal

Carefully, I tear the pages into narrow strips, rendering the handwriting on them totally illegible. It is late in the rough days of my first marriage. I'm sitting in my car in the parking lot of a wooded park. A pickup truck of young guys pulls up next to me, ready for a short hike or a cigarette. The driver watches me for a few minutes, then leans out his window, friendly and cheerful. *I bet I know what you're doing.* I make the mistake of looking up. *I bet that's your diary, isn't it?* Chuckles to his friends. *That's what girls do, they write in 'em and then tear 'em up.* I give him a cool look that almost acknowledges his accuracy, almost gives away my complicity in his sense of humor. Then I go on tearing up strips of my diary for the dumpster at the edge of the lot.

The Moon is Telling Stories Again

rocking the sea to sleep, murmuring over
the sound of a tide drawn up like a blanket.

The sea is its deep plaything. It has heard
of a sister moon, once spinning in unison, then
colliding, carving cliffs on the moon's far side.

The night has heard the Saga of Hector's fall,
which trail leads to the cave of paintings, how stars
began to dance. The night has heard them all.

We hope the moon won't reveal things we've done
in the dark – chocolates stolen from a child's pocket,
wordless betrayals committed on its watch.

The moon has heard, but does not repeat, the legend
of Eve, a story we believe is ours: Adam falling
asleep by the river, then yielding his rib to a myth.

Just as Earth slept, then woke to watch its moon,
newly shaken loose, smuggling tales into its orbit.
Almost ready to speak.

Case Studies

∾

In a green hospital corridor a man says *We are hoping*
   against hope, as if describing Hope
  tilting against itself, two Furies on Olympus

wagering against each other's spells
    while cells multiply beneath them, filling
  his wife's body with wild thistles.

He wagers on drops of poison, slow rain
   falling on buds.

∾

In a nearby woods, a lost child finds an old chair
   in a thicket
  and waits for the witch to appear.

His parents, rigid as caged animals, spill their hopes
   before news cameras. The father

thinks secretly of sacrifices he might make. Cigars.
  A mistress. Himself.

∾

A woman runs down the sidewalk, cursing and striking
   at street lamps, shouting a man's name

over and over. As we pass by we cannot tell
if she has come here, disheveled as a banshee,

from his grave site, his betrayal, or his failure
         once again to kiss her goodbye.

Tomorrow I will leave my house, hungry
         for coffee and a muffin, my bones
    and blood intact. I will choose not to think
of tripping at the top of the steep stairwell.

There are no poisons to which
    I cannot imagine myself immune.

The memory of my father's random fragile
    artery is folded away,
        like family linens in a trunk.

            ℘

We move on, though on certain days we are sure
        we hear omens. Rattle of runes
    cast beneath the oak. Rumor
of a sword with our name on its blade.

Somewhere a black tornado finger flicks a man
        across his neighbor's field,
    an earthquake's crevice
opens between our children's feet.

            ℘

Still, we take heart, remembering
          that when the winter solstice has passed,
      except for the occasional mystery of an eclipse,

the turtle who carries the sun
         across the sky on her back
has not faltered yet.

Held to Account

by the ghosts who slouch at the foot of my 3 AM bed. Two marriages, neither lasted. But oh, those two sons from the first, the families they've created, how they've gladdened my life. *And how did you stay on such good terms with both husbands?* the ghosts ask. Early lessons in forever goodbyes. How to find good, let go of bad. Always, we had hiking trails, songs to listen to, dishes to cook. Always a garden to plant and tend. Always water: swift or still, salty or fresh, white-capped or reflecting guardian trees. Always the moon above, pulling, releasing the tides as I traveled. Always, my footprint: scattered in gravel, in loamy soil, yielding thorns and blossoms.

Site Lines

At his tripod my father surveys a field. Hands clasped
behind him, legs plumb-line straight.

The snapshot's borders show his boundaries,
fine and sharp as draftsman's strokes.

Beyond him is unmarked space. If I prop his picture
on the mantel, then step back,

his contour becomes a faded chalk line. Let's say
I keep moving, circle the earth backward,

a cheerful tourist, fluttering map in hand,
plotting routes behind me.

Shall I pretend surprise when all my calculations
lead me back to him?

As if I never thought to see his face or back again. As if
I could stop my endless survey of his world.

CASTILLO DI MONTEGUFONI

Of the stone lion, I know only his paws.
The low pedestal on which he sat
is now nearly claimed by the slow tides
of Tuscan earth.

Head, ribs, haunches lie beneath the grasses
of a lost terrace. Buried as well, the artisan
who carved him, the workers who hauled him
here in a cart, set his statue just below
the shell-thick grotto.

Time sleeps in layers of light on stone,
in tangled vines. Nine hundred years
of footsteps across the courtyard,
shuffles and clicks of pigeons.
The clatter of leaves.

UNBOUND

Through December's grey flannel dawn, the fox:
a long low streak of russet,
a slant eye tilted toward the window
cold between us.
His blurred shape
burns a meteor through the yard.

Flame's too pale a word
for his crimson path.
He carves a swale through winterweed,
slips behind the shed,
shimmies through the fence,
up to the woods behind the church.

I could follow him. I could
grow red fur.

SLIVERS OF GREEN

The Sense of the World

You made sense of the world for me. My sister's voice, many years ago when we were discussing our growing up years. *I sure was a brat in those days.* She was sometimes, and I was in charge of her. I was teaching myself to make sense of it all as well. Why the nuns at our school wore habits. Why our mother went to work in an office every morning. Why she came home cranky at night, ready for her first drink. I explained the deafening roar of B-52 bombers overhead every afternoon: they were flying back to the nearby air force base after a practice run of mid-air refueling.

When she was very young I was her protector, although later I sometimes joined the older cousins when they teased her. Now no one can give her back a world that makes sense. Her neurons have turned against her, parts of her brain are stiff and plaque-y. We look at old photos together. She recognizes some of the people, none of the houses or landscapes until I name them, and then she tries to tell me what happened there.

SURVIVAL GUIDE

Each of us does what she must.
A praying mantis bit me
in the garden this morning.
just an inch from my left nipple,
as I reached to brush
dead blossoms from the azaleas.

I try to imagine the sound
her mate will hear
when she neatly snaps off his head:
a last metallic click that vibrates
throughout his carapace,
as her mandibles steady his neck.
Thank you for the babies. Now goodbye.

In the shed, it is time to kill
the Brown Recluse spider, her egg-fat
belly adorned with a painted hourglass
shaped just like a dainty corset.
I apologize to her. We women
just want a place to hatch our young,
and then, a bite to eat.

Going Under

Air Florida crash, Washington
D.C., January 1982

In the television's glow, blue as a sunlit glacier,
the flight attendant appeared over and over.
Gaffed by spotlights, on a slab of ice knocked loose
when the plane plunged into the river.

She lay half-stunned amid chunks of metal.
Moved her arms as if to swim through ice and air,
muscles recalling an old survival lesson. She could
do nothing for passengers waiting in their seats,
cold fingers too stiff to loosen seatbelts.

In a darkened house we were studying other ways
to drown, most often in silence. By the second day
we knew her story's end: onlooker with a rope,
frigid hauling in, numbed feet touching ground again.

We went on – the way two children might stand
at the end of a dock, each nudging with a toe
some toy toward the edge until finally it's lost
to deep water. I envied her that rescuing rope,
imagined gripping instead of letting go.

ARMOR

Book on evolution

        Carapace

      beetle behind the stove

            lobster

homo sapiens

skin   fur   coat

cave

      lean-to

          house

shelter

   safety

      protection

car   mobile carapace

armor

      yours   being right

      mine   being blameless

RISING AND CONVERGING

She leans forward, like a woman
in a Chagall,
staring down at the life
she'll leave, decomposing
one room at a time.
Kitchen drawers full of knives,
charred meat odor
clinging to the drapes,
walls stained with quarrels.

Rising late on summer days,
she peels sleep away
like the skin of an orange.
Outside, lime green shoots
pretend it's spring. She reaches
down to run her hand along
crepe myrtle trunks.
The neighbor's dog
still barks across the fence.

She wants
to lift the house,
to pull the basement loose.
If she could hold it
to her body, the chimney
pressed against her ribs,
she'd rock its frame.

THINGS LEFT BEHIND

Through the window, a landscape after rain,
the charcoal cat now drinking from a puddle in the street.

I look up from my book, wonder if she tastes
an essence of the bird who preened there hours ago.

This world is full of shapes that echo things not there.
The matted grass, for instance, when the lion rises from sleep.

Or your gloves lying on the chair, their remembered shape of hands.
I find comments in the book you left, penciled in the margins.

My finger traces *Yes!* or *I disagree*, as if to touch your skin.
I hold you in thought until you're here, waiting like a cat
circling a saucer, waiting for the taste of fresh-poured cream.

LATITUDE

Pretend that in another life I swerve, drive off a cliff,
never reach the market, never make you soup.
Or say a witness finds you in an alley, left for dead,

while next door in the cafe, a man is eating salmon;
he resembles you remarkably. Arriving with their chairs
to join him, the separated twins rejoice, sit with ankles

crossed like algebraic plots. When you leave,
look over your shoulder, see the particles of light
reflect unruly opposites.

You thought I'd left for Venice. I am waiting
in a cabin, holding lilacs. Now we are spinning heel
to toe, like Fred and Ginger in the ballroom mirror.
Reeling through our next fox trot.

Debris

From last year's birdhouse,
the song sparrow plucks twigs
and fluff. She sits on the fence

and spits the discards to the ground
as if with a small curse.
One white feather she saves,

carries it like a talisman to the bush
in my neighbor's yard,
ready to begin weaving again.

For my part, I have discarded
your last flannel shirt. I've straightened
the dog ears you folded on book pages.

Remembering your aftershave,
I fling open windows,
burn incense while I scrub the floor.

My heart cracks like a windfall limb.
I do everything
but spit on the ground.

SOUNDINGS

I heard of a man with an ear so finely tuned
he could tell the length of pine needles on a tree
from the sound of wind moving through its limbs.

Perhaps like me, he'd moved along a stream,
listened for the perfect pitch of water
running over stones, a treble that echoed a creek

from an earlier life. Light notes ringing like bells.
He would know why, beyond the obvious,
San Francisco's morning traffic sounds so hushed,

so *foggy*, compared to Washington's pneumatic drone.
I thought today of the deep-sky summer night
when I stood with you on asphalt not yet cooled.

Crickets clattered: the sound of a thousand bamboo sticks.
Our voices, our new words. No one but us to hear
the French horn whistle of a freight train,
wrapping us in waves.

PLEASE

On warm spring nights in Vermont, volunteers count peepers, wood frogs, newts (drab or spotted). With flashlights they lead four- and five-toed salamanders across country roads, protecting them as they race toward ancient mating ponds. Stragglers become dark stains on asphalt.

Trowel in hand, I stepped outside today to crumble earthen clods, ready beds for seedlings. I bent the moonflower vine's first tendril toward its trellis. Crows shook the treetops with alarms as a hawk approached.

I remember a climbing class in West Virginia: the man on belay next to me (cramped, sweat-spotted), splayed across sheer rock as tightly as a skink. The instructor, offering to point out the waiting toe-hold. The man's soft-breathed *Oh, please,* all our human fear and gratitude, whispered into stone.

GONE

my sister flinches
    from a shadow that follows her
through the house
rubbing like an eraser
blurring as she goes

sometimes just around the edges
    sometimes
with a swipe that rubs
the past from sight

debris
    of names   of scenes
falling   at her feet

then   nothing

and I – who've always led her
    through this world
    sending messages
from the path ahead –

I follow clumsily
    losing
        the parts of me that once
were parts of her

Runway

We are forty minutes outside Denver
when the blonde in black and muted gold
saunters through the plane. By chance I follow her,

and in the noisy loo I find her scribbled pages:
an address book torn into shreds, discarded
while the bulkhead roared around her.

I rummage through a sheaf of clues.
Names changed, crossed out, new numbers
signifying moves to distant towns. I see

Des Moines and *Santa Cruz*, places I have been,
and wonder why she tore these up.

Down the slide of clouds we ride,
suspended in our silver tube. We land
in a familiar place we've never seen before.

Like confetti from a shredder, we scatter
last week's hours. We think we have escaped.
We love our lightweight luggage.

RECONCILIATIONS

San Francisco was, as always, colder than I'd expected when we deplaned. The second day we were there we located the Sunset District and Northwood Drive. In no time, as if time had not elapsed, I recognized the first house I'd known, framed on its corner lot by trees, two large pillars at either end of the wide front porch. Hesitantly, I rang the door bell but no one answered. I wasn't disappointed. I looked around at the shape of the house settled into its garden. I recognized the places where my father took family photos; where I watched my mother plant her rock garden; where I sat on the edge of the porch and fell in three-year-old love with my handsome blond half brother, nineteen years my senior, while he washed his car at the curb.

Later I had the same sensation – an unexpected wave of warm familiarity – in front of the apartment house on Sacramento Street, a block or so down from Lafayette Park where I learned how to roll down a grassy hill, how to tie daisy chains. In that city of hills, fog, sun on water, I sensed my mother next to me, in her good-mothering years: holding me just enough, teaching me just enough, at just the right seasons, about how to escape and survive, how to find her again in those lessons, now that I'd finally come back.

Abrams Falls
for JR

It's a three beer hike you said, just as Tibetans calculate
how many cups of tea are required for a journey.
So you pulled our wagon up the trail, passed out beer as we
hiked. Rhododendron, laurel blooming everywhere we looked.

From the top of the falls you dove, never thinking
to test the depth, of course, and I couldn't watch,
as with other gauntlets you'd swaggered through.

You surfaced safely, pleased as a seal.

At the far end of the garden, the laurels
we brought home that day are thick with blossoms.

I think of gray ashes wedged between rocks, caught
when our sons emptied the mason jar you'd specified,
your chosen songs loud on the tape deck, as they poured loose
what remained of you, into the falls once more.

Reprieve

These nights we are awakened
from uneasy dreams
by the song

of the mockingbird,
when he's done with chasing
the neighbor's cat.

His cascading notes
recall perfect nights past:
children sleeping

while we sipped our wine,
rhythm of sprinklers
on darkened alfalfa fields,

driving alone in a coral dawn, across
the Golden Gate Bridge, monarchs
of all the suspension cables
we could see.

GOOD OMENS IN BONES

Amphibian Lives

Winter dawn an hour away, Orion chasing
Venus through the sky. We follow the smell
of chlorine, wet footprints on tiles,
stumble to the pool. All the waters
we've ever known wait there.

As if in amniotic sacs
of dreams, we float. Like ancestral
fish, newly gilled, we stroke
and breathe, stroke and breathe,

end a lap, tuck and turn. We scatter
parrot fish among coral stalks,
surf the halls of Roman baths,
backstroke high tides through
a grotto's passage.

We emerge to shower and dress.
Sleek haired, our nylon bags zipped tight,
upright. Tucked beneath our jackets,
the vestiges of fins.

Strokes of White

The poet-philosopher writes, *This is your time to harvest,*
to sort cupboards full of memories and keepsake scraps.

The senior living pamphlet says, *Discard. divest,*
donate and downsize; take only golf clubs
and yoga pants to your next abode.

I miss my silent seatmate from the flight to Tucson,
the one who listened to my story, then deplaned
without a nod or shrug. I sidestep helpful friends
running after me, returning a shared regret

like a fallen glove. Almost glad it takes a village,
or at least a quorum of my book club, to remember
Humphrey Bogart's wife.

At 3 a.m. I visit wakeful dreams, filled with relics:
the Model A jalopies and battered Buicks of my youth,
all those crew-cut boys, the awkward words we spoke.

At 4 a.m. I scrutinize paths not taken.

Last week I learned a new word: *virga.*
It illuminates these days for me,
describes soft wisps of ice or rain
that fall from clouds but never reach

the earth. They trail, suspended blessings,
gauzy strokes of white beneath their mother cloud.

The *never reaching* of the virga is what speaks
to me. Memories uncaught, my waiting life
which lingers, unfinished rain.

SEQUENTIAL NAVIGATION

There was a spot in the middle of the lake
  far enough out for us to know
  there was no point turning back.
Blank and rippled surface, absence
  of boot prints or blazes on trees,
just the opposite shore, visible, waiting.

Leaning back at last week's dinner table,
  pleased that we'd come together again:
  my sons, their families,
the dearest people in my world.

Before I dreamed them as boys:
  their father, whistling while I climbed
  onto the back of his Vespa,
setting out from Garmisch to Rome.

In Europe, because we'd planned this trip
  while playing canasta in my college dorm,
  listening to Michel LeGrande's, "Holiday in Rome."
Canasta in that particular college dorm

because of the argument with my mother, the first
  I'd ever won. How newly brave I felt,
  With words in my heart from my high school
chemistry teacher: *You'll make it as a scholar,*
but never as a chemist.

On the lake, if we could handle contentment,
      we'd think of the gravelly shore ahead
      ready to ease us up to granite hand-holds.
We'd know that halfway across meant
we were as good as there. We'd float
      on our back. dream at the sky.

CHALLENGE

There is a crack in everything.
That's how the light gets in.
Leonard Cohen

You think
    you're traveling alone
    armored in a trance

Pretending no one else is here

Then why the pair of sneakers
    hanging by their laces
    from a tree limb?

Who's behind the fluttering tie-back curtains?
    The laundry on the line?

Where is the woman going,
    waiting with her paper
    for the bus?

You'd like a pane
    of wavy leaded glass,
    a scrim to muffle curiosity.

You think you're traveling alone

until you learn this world
     will pull you back,
     hatch its story
in every field and ditch

dare you to forget it.

Under Leo

In the thrall of the lion
we gauge the weight
of melons, of peaches,
of hair damp
with ocean salt.

It is time to go out,
to sit in a field
on a warm rock,
or on a lip of earth
near the edge of the woods.

Time to visit
the vegetable stand,
under the pine trees
whose needles spindle
the heavy air.

Time to become
a slim vertical line
against the constant
of the sea
and its horizon.

Or to be drawn
like thin brush strokes
along the twilight beach,
kites and children
reeled in, the day

withdrawing itself
across the sand.

Things a Sundial Won't Tell You

I've come to believe
the natural life of a garden
is twenty years,
give or take an arid season:
the span of time I've lived here.

Above their deck, the newlyweds
next door have raised a blue canvas tent,
a second sky. In less than twenty days,
their landscape artisan installed
a pebbled fountain, lattice, twelve azaleas.

Across a wooden fence, thirty feet
and fifty years from them,
I'm awash in greenery, planted on my own,
dug in with the gritty nerve
of the newly divorced.

Now all of it needs pruning.
Every spring, shrubs want lifting,
tossing out, a letting in of light.

Ten years ago at the garden's half-life,
you arrived, bringing love and carving
a newcomer's path through the trees.

I've learned why you thrive in autumn,
and I in spring. The way each seedling,

fragile and modest, takes
what it needs from air and soil.
How love becomes sturdy.

It'll Be Easy

I consulted an astrologer during one of those lazily curious seasons between busyness and loose ends, in my sixtieth year. After I gave him my birth date over the phone, he consulted many books and charts and I then had a session in which he interpreted a complicated diagram of planets and houses. I did not have a very focused chart: Pisces' dreaminess flirting with Sagittarius' optimistic charms, Neptune very strong, few Earth signs. Fortunately, the Virgo mother I'd mentioned, to anchor me and instill some practicality. Mars in Pluto signified integrative mental powers; but would that count after Pluto's planetary status was revoked?

When he'd finished telling me what I'd arrived in this world with, I told him that in those days I was living on my own for the first time, furnishing a house, building a profession, a new life, friendships, a large garden. I asked him if he saw another man ever in my life. He leaned back and smiled. *Oh yes, give it a couple of years. You won't even have to work at it. It'll be easy. You'll just turn and he'll be sitting right there next to you.* And that's where you were, sitting next to me at the long conference table, talking about poems.

SKYLIGHT

While you read to me I watch
a spider swing between two rafters,
spinning in a trembling world.

The skylight above us mirrors
our pale feet on the sheets,
holds the moon in a glass.

Earlier, rain spilled down its surface,
while across the room the drops' reflections
slithered down the wall like watered silk.

In Medieval times, men believed
looking at the moon through glass
would bring bad luck. If so,

we're happily doomed, lying here
like pagans. gazing in contentment
at the night's deep eye.

For you I will make up a dream.
In it you will find me for the first
and thousandth times: sunlight,

moonlight on our shoulders,
brushing them like hands.
Our words will fly around
the room like origami birds.

What the Geese Saw

                    when they tipped
their flat grey eyes to look up at the bridge
wasn't bread crumbs falling, only me
looking down, shrugging at their feathered
questions, and you staring up the river
with great purpose.

Our eyes not meeting, the way we'd been
avoiding each other all week. Each word
a stone ready to strike water, shatter
our reflections as we tried to pull
the edges of our story together again.

Downstream we found the lake,
its two great herons etched
in narrow blue calligraphy
against the mud flats. *Look!* you cried:
first one, then the other lifted,
their wings beating in rhythm
like oars against gravity.

We watched, then turned to one another.
This is how it might become for us:
each wing stroke, each moment,
holding its opposite as well,
its news of the way forward
passing back and forth between us.

Marrow

Because I liked the look of the tiramisu
on the plate of the girl sitting by the window,
we've slipped into this cafe, eluded

the moon, its July-hot eye waiting
at the end of the block. Now our cranky
waiter gestures his approval

with platters of osso buco, good omens
in the bones he's heaped on our plates,
dense with tongue-slick marrow.

In the background Tony Bennett croons,
a maudlin uncle asking for a kiss
to build a dream on. I think of the couple

near Lucca, kissing by a wall, the old man
passing by and smiling, his cart filled deep
with grapes on their way to the winery.

Soon the poetic lion of contentment
will make his way between the tables,
soft-pawed, ready to follow us home

to our room under the eaves. Beyond
the floating skylight, the milky way
becomes the marrow of the moon.

Now draw the curtains, as perhaps the couple
did in Lucca hours ago.

An Algorithm for Time

At the airport I am impatient,
explaining that what I resisted most
about the existentialists
was their insistence that we're stuck
with passing *through* time, or watching *it*
pass us. Enlightenment in a hamster's wheel.

We watch cabbies lined up for fares,
wrestling minutes into laughter,
then into quarrels, until a business traveler
appears, defines their destination.

We take the back road home, shunning
a gridlocked interstate. Motion, or its illusion,
comforts more than distance.

Today the equinox has come and gone,
leaves flash red. At dusk I sit
among the cohort of my dreams.

They bring up memory, that stout suitcase
packed with scenes. These days shine
and I have come to join them, in spite
of seasons when I didn't think I would.

Leeward Nights

bougainvillea wakes me
 rustling against stones

swish of taffeta
nights in the city

in the bar a woman says
when she walks by, men hear
the sound of satin sheets

I have taken down
my mirrors
I let your eyes design me

our bodies lie together
two bolts of folded silk

THE TRAIN TO NEW YORK CITY

Aftermath of ribbons and carols. Discarded
trees and tinsel. Rough woods beyond
the windows. Sway mimics the rhythm
of wheels beneath us, vibrating against
distracted bones. Fields gone past
autumn gold to winter drab.

Two hawks have joined the clouds. They wheel
above, then dive with me inside my thoughts.
Forty miles beyond the cards and cookies, I send
a blessing to the winter-coated man hunched over
by a truck in Baltimore, send blessings to
the solitary girl across the aisle, thumbing texts
and frowning.

I reach out, touch your arm as you read.
Slide my fingers across the softness
of your sweater. Interrupt your busyness,
coax you to turn and see what is in my eyes.

About the Author

Ann Rayburn was born in California in 1934. Poetry called to her early; she wrote her first poem at six and can recall all but one line of it. She received a degree in English from Stanford, where she was accepted as an undergraduate into the university's creative writing program. A move to the east coast and a mid-life focus on career development, plus raising two sons, led to thirty-five years' practice as a psychotherapist and to an intermittent hiatus in writing. Now retired, she lives with her partner, Jeremy Taylor, in Falls Church, Virginia, where she writes, gardens, and keeps track of her four grandchildren.

www.ingramcontent.com/pod-product-compliance
Lightning Source LLC
Chambersburg PA
CBHW020912090426
42736CB00008B/604